Daughter Tongue

Poems by

Joanne Mallari

Cover design by Shay Culligan

ISBN: 978-1-952326-35-6

Kelsay Books
502 South 1040 East, A-119
American Fork, Utah, 84003

Daughter Tongue

For Jude and Judy Mallari

Acknowledgments

I am grateful to the editors of the following journals in which these poems first appeared:

Adanna Literary Journal: "After Close"

A-Minor Magazine: "Cluster Chords"

Crab Orchard Review: "At the Jelly Donut"

Haight Ashbury Literary Journal: "Acquisition, Language," "Laundry Date"

The MacGuffin: "Ode to Videoke," "Reacquaintance"

The Meadow: "On *Duende*," "On Windy Hill"

Palimpsest: "Abecedarian on Forgetting," "Bilingual Naiveté"

The Vitni Review: "Origami"

Many thanks to Steve Gehrke, Gailmarie Pahmeier, Ann Keniston, James Mardock, Daniel Enrique Pérez, Jared Stanley, and Chris Coake for their mentorship and support during the development of this manuscript. Thanks to Kelsay Books for the opportunity to publish my first chapbook. Immense gratitude to my writing community near and far: Sunny Solomon, Brandy Burgess, Matthew Baker, Olivia Soule, Justin Williams, Raluca Balasa, Christina Camarena, Rachel Chimits, Molly Gutman, AnnElise Hatjakes, Nate Perry, Brian Rowe, Casey Bell, Isabelle Lang, Garnet Sanford, Logan Seidl, and Michelle Wait. Thanks to Nevada Humanities and Sierra Arts Foundation for the opportunity to share and practice my craft in Northern Nevada. My deepest gratitude to my parents, Jude and Judy Mallari, who supported me all along.

Contents

Bilingual Naiveté

I.

I learned to make love to a woman
by loosening my tongue
underneath the Shoe Tree
on Highway 50—
a monument to tongues
trapped under laces.

Making love is exposing
your first language—
words you held down
with double-knotted bows
because you couldn't stand
to show their sound.

My first felony was telling
my father, over the phone,
her name. *Oh,* he said,
the sound falling
like a curtain
on a scene
gone wrong.

She loosened my tongue
beneath a curtain of shoes,
the kiss muscle memory
unfolding—like when,
in a parking lot,
a Jehovah's Witness
spoke to me in Tagalog,
and the words, trapped,
unlaced themselves.

II.

I go into muscle memory
like saying Catholic prayers.
Some prayers cannot be uttered
alone but next to someone
who knows the words you don't.

First point of similarity:
she keeps a rosary hanging
over her rearview mirror.

I meditate on her lips,
follow each open and close
like a string of *Hail Marys*.

I can't recall, between
decades, what to recite.

I touch her in the ways
I know how. She fills in
where I don't.

Acquisition, Language

When Lola visits, we share
the language of crochet stitches:
chain four, connect, chain three,
double crochet, repeat times six.

Under, over, and through the loops
I guide the hook without stopping,
the way I've watched Lola do it
since I was little. She looks over
my shoulder, and I wonder if she
approves of the cadence in my hands
as I chain variegated thread.

Blue, green, purple, blue—rows
of ocean-colored thread ripple outward
like the sea that comes between us
when Lola goes back to the Philippines.

Because we do not see each other often,
we try to immerse ourselves in the details
that make up our lives. As usual, Lola
begins the pattern. *Kamusta na?*
she asks. How do I tell her that
I can understand better than I speak?

I hung Tagalog in the closet
when I was seven and left it
like an unwanted coat, left
its mouthy vowels and velar
nasals in an attempt to disinherit
the accent of my mother tongue.

Chain four, connect, chain three,
double crochet, repeat times six.
I know this language from all
the time I spent immersing
my hands in Lola's rhythm
and syntax, connecting basic
stitches to form intricate patterns
in the space before she leaves.

I don't want her to think
that I have undone my roots
as easily as one can unravel
the rows of stitches.

On *Duende*

I tell him that desire is the inside
       of a cathedral, which is ornate,
which is fragile, which is too big
       to fill, which doesn't
stay filled with the same people.
       Even the windows

depend on the weather. See there,
       that first panel
of stained glass? Seven days
       of creation told in fragments
of warm and cool hues,
       mounted on a wall

as if at any time
       one piece could migrate,
affix itself to another,
       make a hybrid.
Did I mean it with the woman
       who came before?

On the porch, with the light
       blinking, she traced
a finger behind my ear,
       compelled my spine to cave,
and the heart made room,
       but I don't give him all

these pieces. I tell him, instead,
       about the wonder of lamp light
as it comes through blinds, falls
       in strips across
his torso, moves me to trace
       from neck to navel.

Hours from now we'll wake up
        to blue-gray
because this side of the house
        does not face morning sun.

On Windy Hill

If there is something to desire, there will be something to regret.
—*Vera Pavlova*

I listen for the sound of sighs, for why
they call it Windy Hill. You reach
over, rub my hands, and I wonder if,
this time, it will be enough for you.
Lights pulse like Morse code in the city
below. They say we are living. They say
we can see. They signal us to stop
or keep going—we can count the lights
later if we take the time. The roads, too,
are pulsing, oxygenated by the fear
and longing of whoever is traveling
at this hour. Down there, someone
is thinking of how to slow time.
Another is thinking of how to make it
go faster, bypass the awkward middle.
You pull the driver's seat back, recline,
motion for me to lay on top. I want
to prove that I don't lack affection
the way you say I do in public spaces.
You've never been one to care about
spectators. If the rain comes while
we're here, you'll tell me to run
with you—run like there won't be
another, like there will be a drought.

Origami

I am too timid / to make love
I keep my want / hovering
like rest notes / before a bridge

Always I hear / the right person
will make / for a new kind
of music / I let her show me

I try to forget / the other hands
placed upon me / in a bathroom
or a parking garage / Instead

of feeling gospel / soar inside me
I relive the sound / of a tree crashing
with no one else / around to hear.

My body / pulls back / gives away
the fear / She stops / cradles me
on the floor / I cross my arms

and legs / folding / into myself
like a square of paper / trying
to become a crane / She tells me

to release / let go / the shame
The underside / of patterned paper
is a blank space /

In Contrast

I. Courtship

Lola's stories begin: "I met him—
        your *lolo*—at the *Flores de Mayo*
                festival, when I was young

and beautiful." She points at a portrait
        of herself at eighteen, hanging above
                a cabinet of dolls whose faces, too,

will never wrinkle, always resemble
        Maria Clara, archetypal Filipina.
                I imagine the young woman

stepping down from the frame to take
        Lolo's hand, a gesture forbidden
                because he is a poor sailor, and she

the daughter of a plantation owner.
        He leads with a firm hold that says
                he is ready to waltz her over class

lines; he intends to come back over
        and over, and that's when he slips
                the flower in her hair,

which she preserves twice:
        first by posing with it, then
                by pressing petals inside her Bible.

II. Dating

In the context of your *cariño*
I flounder:

    Te quiero

        Thank you

  What?

      Yes

I guess I don't know
    what to say. I don't know
what to do with your lips
    coming down on mine.

Did I tell you when I saw
    snow for the first time,
        caught off guard wearing
the wrong thing? I turn my head

to one side, praise the only
    flores here, hanging
from your rearview
mirror:

    Nice lei.

    Thanks?

In my head you ask if I know
      the best vantage point for looking up
          at Orion's Belt. You ask me

what songs I like to slow dance to.
      In my head this ends with a goodnight
          kiss, but first we talk until

our breath fogs the windows—
      until no one can see inside.

Abecedarian on Forgetting

After leaving your mother tongue
behind, you wondered how you
could name love and loss,
define coming and going.
Each word that came to mind marked
full assimilation to the dominant culture.
Going home, you told your mother
how futile it was to hang on to words
in Tagalog. Sometimes adrenaline
jogged your memory; more often, relatives
kindly switched to English,
leaving you to puzzle
moments long after the fact: was there
not a better way to say it? You knew
over thousands of words once:
pamangkin (niece); *maliit* (little);
questions demanded a *sagot*. Other words
recalled Spanish roots: *misa,*
syempre, Diyos, but not
tayo, which means "us" or "to stand."
Under one language the other lies,
vamping like a pianist
who waits for you to start singing.
Except for the American accent,
you could pass for who you were before you
zoned your tongue for reconstruction.

After close

the DJ asks me to sing one
we both know by Priscilla Ahn.

I say yes because I love
the resonance of an empty bar,

how words search for an ear
to land on, and I can untangle

myself from prying eyes, but even
this is uneasy. Underneath

the sappy crooning, I wonder
how it worked out for Priscilla,

taking long walks in the dark
and asking God who we're supposed

to be when nothing is constant
and everything turns—an hour

into a day, a rule into a reason
to do it anyway. From the patio,

two stars pierce the sky like diamond
studs in her cartilage. We inhabit

the space between the worry and
the what-if. She leans in, never mind

I haven't—hadn't—kissed a woman before.

Cluster Chords

When we were young, Mama made us
wear red after loved ones died—
otherwise, they'd come in dreams,

convince us to cross over. Now, I think,
more frightening than seeing the deceased
in our sleep is being seen while making

love. Imagine: the ancestors watch you
bare your skin, so carefully covered
around Catholic kin. I wouldn't expose

my shoulders then, am still a self-conscious
lover. I leave my shirt on at times,
lose bravado stroking her thighs, to think

they'd see me as I really am. Even the blinds
can admit the dead, let them see into
the dark. For the living I lie by omission,

cross out letters the way I would
for an erasure poem, until all that's left
are the words they want to see: underneath

I kiss another woman back. Her lips
loose monarchs in me. Each breath feels
like loud steps in an empty church—

the sound rising to the loft, knocking
on the confessional. I pray for more of her
whose tongue draws dissonant chords

from me. Under cover we fall in love
with the sound of longing and restraint,
clashing until we can see ripples in air.

Laundry Date

We spend our anniversary counting down
the minutes until the cycle is finished.
Nothing says friendship like watching
each other's panties tumble in the dryer
while a priest recites Mass on the television
behind us. No matter which way we turn
our heads, it is all ritual. If today is typical,
the man who sells tamales will stop by
and ask us if we'd like chicken or beef,
y ¿Cuántos quiere? A Jehovah's Witness
will pass out pamphlets, and the woman
who works at the counter will step outside
for a cigarette. We only know these people
by gesture, and I wonder if they know us
by ours—like pressing our hands against
the dryers to make sure they are still
heating up. If we got to know one another
by more than just our waiting, washing,
and folding, if we got to know one another
by more than our leaning, standing, waiting,
we'd reveal our inability to sort our selves,
like how her thoughts in Spanish bleed into
her thoughts in English, and my love of God
bleeds into my love for another woman.

Ode to Videoke

Safe zone; ballad buffet;
cousins only; private party;
little booze—not enough
to shock the *lolas* and the *titas*.

I sing Tagalog, sing English.
Mariah, Maroon 5—
it's all in the book.
Now Mama knows why
I go all the time. In the U.S.

I prefer a little joint
where people come
as strangers, leave
as friends. No better glue

than Midori and Madonna.
There I told a drag queen—
6'5" with a purple wig—
how stunning she looked
in stilettoes. She belted

"All that Jazz," left a trail
of words on karaoke slips
like fortune cookies:
The beginning is you.
The middle is you.

The end is you.
Am I the someone
who'll one day show me
how to love? Sometimes
I think I swing a certain way.
If love is on a swing,

does it come back the other way?
I sing beneath rainbow flags
and church banners, too.
Lady Gaga, Ave Maria—
hits of the past, hits of the present:

as it was in the beginning,
is now and shall be
world without end.
When I think "world without end,"
I picture metaphors for the lines

that we straddle:
Venn diagram; mash-up;
novel told in vignettes.
Cup of chamomile citrus—

the calm beneath the zest.
Crossover; triple threat;
soprano-turned-pop:
my voice a revolving door,
my heart the disc jock.

At the Jelly Donut

What a dollar buys: sugar twist
or chocolate bar. Sprinkled

or jelly-filled. I come here still,
fixated on things a dollar can't

repair: broken dryers next door,
letter missing from Mega L undry,

worn brake pads, last break-up.
I write you off from a round

metal seat chiseled with hearts,
initials. On what I think a dollar

can fix: I leave a trace of myself
in the plastic donation box—

four quarters for the March of Dimes.
Checkout charity feeds my insta-hero

complex. What is love but a series
of deposits, pennies piling on top

of nickels on top of dimes until
we die or forget? In the beginning

we exchanged words to flatter,
paid compliments in kind.

You taught me *hermosa.* I gave
you *matapang.* I replay this version

of us beneath the sign flashing
Open 24 Hours. Later you became

the Post-it, the voicemail, the text,
and I the candle covering the scent

of "Love you. See you later."
Your leaving smells richer

than it tastes. You leave a small
digital trace. The last I heard

from you via messenger: *No
for now.* You show me *dolor.*

I'd tell you this is *lungkot,*
a quiet lament like folding

a napkin carefully before
throwing it away.

Reacquaintance

—After Derek Walcott

After love, I avoid all roses.
I buy hydrangeas and other blooms
whose names are too mouthy
to spark memory.

I move my lips to alstromeria,
a sound like a sewing machine
stitching faster than I can by hand,
then petal for none other than
the stranger who was my self.

I give back the names she called me
(too syrupy to list here). I reach
into the fibers of my self, stitch
new sounds together, and listen:

a feast brews here, a gust of vowels
with no consonants to stop them,
the way sopranos sustain the "eh"
in heaven. I sing a descant above.
I sing a moniker flowering.

A time will come when the syllables
are still, then I will greet the new self
arriving, call her by a name only I
can form my lips around.

About the Author

Joanne Mallari is a teaching assistant professor at the University of Nevada, Reno. She served as the 2019 Nevada Humanities Poet in Residence, and she advocates for equitable access to arts education. She contributes book reviews at *bookinwithsunny.com*.

www.ingramcontent.com/pod-product-compliance
Lightning Source LLC
Chambersburg PA
CBHW071753090426
42738CB00011B/2669